THIS BOOK BELONGS TO

SUNDERLAND A.F.C.

Name: Age:

Favourite player:

2017·2018
My Predictions...   Actual...

Sunderland's final position:

Sunderland's top scorer:

Championship winners:

Championship top scorer:

FA Cup winners:

EFL Cup winners:

Written by Rob Mason

A TWOCAN PUBLICATION

©2017. Published by twocan under licence from Sunderland AFC.

Every effort has been made to ensure the accuracy of information within this publication but the publishers can not be held responsible for any errors or omissions. Views expressed are those of the authors and do not necessarily represent those of the publishers or the football club. All rights reserved.

ISBN: 978-1-911502-23-4

£8.99

PICTURE CREDITS: Action Images, Getty Images, Press Association.

CONTENTS

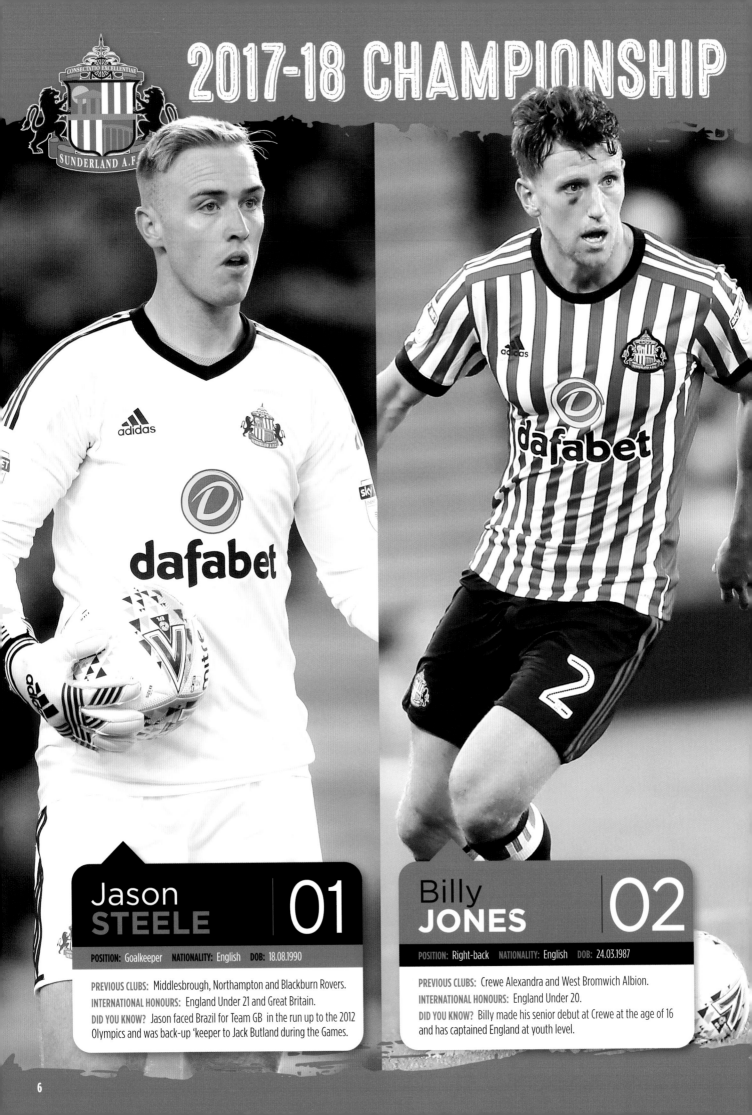

SUNDERLAND A.F.

Jason STEELE | 01

POSITION: Goalkeeper **NATIONALITY:** English **DOB:** 18.08.1990

PREVIOUS CLUBS: Middlesbrough, Northampton and Blackburn Rovers.

INTERNATIONAL HONOURS: England Under 21 and Great Britain.

DID YOU KNOW? Jason faced Brazil for Team GB in the run up to the 2012 Olympics and was back-up 'keeper to Jack Butland during the Games.

Billy JONES | 02

POSITION: Right-back **NATIONALITY:** English **DOB:** 24.03.1987

PREVIOUS CLUBS: Crewe Alexandra and West Bromwich Albion.

INTERNATIONAL HONOURS: England Under 20.

DID YOU KNOW? Billy made his senior debut at Crewe at the age of 16 and has captained England at youth level.

Bryan OVIEDO | 03

POSITION: Left-back   **NATIONALITY:** Costa Rican   **DOB:** 18.01.1990

PREVIOUS CLUBS: Saprissa, Copenhagen, Nordsjaelland and Everton.
INTERNATIONAL HONOURS: Costa Rica.
DID YOU KNOW? Bryan won the Danish league and the cup twice in his time with Copenhagen.

Lee CATTERMOLE | 06

POSITION: Midfielder   **NATIONALITY:** English   **DOB:** 21.03.1988

PREVIOUS CLUBS: Middlesbrough and Wigan Athletic.
INTERNATIONAL HONOURS: England Under 21.
DID YOU KNOW? As a boy, Lee was a member of Sunderland's academy before the Stockton-born player made his name with Middlesbrough.

Paddy McNAIR | 04

POSITION: Midfielder   **NATIONALITY:** Irish   **DOB:** 27.04.1995

PREVIOUS CLUBS: Manchester United.
INTERNATIONAL HONOURS: Northern Ireland.
DID YOU KNOW? Paddy has represented Northern Ireland at every age group from U16 to senior level and he played twice at Euro 2016.

Jonny WILLIAMS | 07

POSITION: Midfielder   **NATIONALITY:** Welsh   **DOB:** 09.10.1993

PREVIOUS CLUBS: Crystal Palace, Ipswich Town, Nottm Forest and MK Dons.
INTERNATIONAL HONOURS: Wales.
DID YOU KNOW? Jonny is on a season-long loan from Crystal Palace where he was Young Player of the Year in 2012-13.

Jack RODWELL | 08

POSITION: Midfielder **NATIONALITY:** English **DOB:** 11.03.1991

PREVIOUS CLUBS: Everton and Manchester City.
INTERNATIONAL HONOURS: England.
DID YOU KNOW? Jack played for Everton Under 18s when he was 14, their reserves at 15 and for the first team in Europe at 16.

Lewis GRABBAN | 11

POSITION: Forward / Winger **NATIONALITY:** English **DOB:** 12.01.1988

PREVIOUS CLUBS: Crystal Palace, Oldham Athletic, Motherwell, Millwall, Brentford, Rotherham United, Bournemouth, Norwich City, Bournemouth (second spell) and Reading.
INTERNATIONAL HONOURS: Jamaica.
DID YOU KNOW? Lewis is on a season-long loan to Sunderland from Bournemouth.

James VAUGHAN | 09

POSITION: Striker **NATIONALITY:** English **DOB:** 14.07.1998

PREVIOUS CLUBS: Everton, Derby County, Leicester City, Crystal Palace, Norwich City, Huddersfield Town, Birmingham City and Bury.
INTERNATIONAL HONOURS: England Under 21.
DID YOU KNOW? James was the youngest player ever to score in the Premier League when he netted for Everton against Crystal Palace when he was only 16 years and 271 days old.

Mika DOMINGUES | 12

POSITION: Goalkeeper **NATIONALITY:** Portuguese **DOB:** 03.08.1991

PREVIOUS CLUBS: Uniao Leiria, Benfica, Benfica B, Atletico and Boavista.
INTERNATIONAL HONOURS: Portugal Under 21.
DID YOU KNOW? Although Mika was born in Switzerland, he represents Portugal and was voted the 2011 U20 World Cup 'keeper of the tournament.

Duncan WATMORE | 14

POSITION: Forward **NATIONALITY:** English **DOB:** 08.03.1994

PREVIOUS CLUBS: Altrincham, Clitheroe and Hibernian.
INTERNATIONAL HONOURS: England Under 21.
DID YOU KNOW? Duncan, who was with Manchester Utd until he was 12, graduated with a first in Economics & Business at Newcastle University.

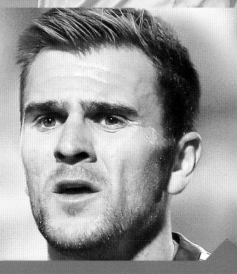

Callum McMANAMAN | 13

POSITION: Winger **NATIONALITY:** English **DOB:** 25.04.1991

PREVIOUS CLUBS: Everton, Wigan Athletic, Blackpool, West Bromwich Albion and Sheffield Wednesday.
INTERNATIONAL HONOURS: England Under 20.
DID YOU KNOW? Callum was 'Man of the Match' in the 2013 FA Cup final when Wigan beat Everton.

Brendan GALLOWAY | 15

POSITION: Left-back **NATIONALITY:** English **DOB:** 17.03.1996

PREVIOUS CLUBS: MK Dons, Everton and West Bromwich Albion.
INTERNATIONAL HONOURS: England Under 21.
DID YOU KNOW? Brendan is on a season-long loan from Everton. He also played in the FA Cup for MK Dons when he was just 15!

John
O'SHEA | 16

POSITION: Centre-back   **NATIONALITY:** Irish   **DOB:** 30.04.1981

PREVIOUS CLUBS: Manchester United, Bournemouth and Antwerp.

INTERNATIONAL HONOURS: Republic of Ireland.

DID YOU KNOW? In his younger days, John played in every position for Manchester United including goalkeeper and centre-forward!

Didier
NDONG | 17

POSITION: Midfielder   **NATIONALITY:** Gabonese   **DOB:** 17.06.1994

PREVIOUS CLUBS: CS Sfaxien and Lorient.

INTERNATIONAL HONOURS: Gabon.

DID YOU KNOW? When he played in Tunisia for Sfaxion, Didier played under Dutch World Cup great Ruud Krol.

Tyias BROWNING | 18

POSITION: Centre-back **NATIONALITY:** English **DOB:** 27.05.1994

PREVIOUS CLUBS: Everton and Preston North End.

INTERNATIONAL HONOURS: None.

DID YOU KNOW? Tyias is on a season-long loan from Everton for whom he made his debut against Liverpool. He can also play at right-back.

Aiden McGEADY | 19

POSITION: Winger **NATIONALITY:** Irish **DOB:** 04.04.1986

PREVIOUS CLUBS: Queen's Park, Celtic, Spartak Moscow, Everton, Sheffield Wednesday and Preston North End.

INTERNATIONAL HONOURS: Republic of Ireland.

DID YOU KNOW? Playing for Simon Grayson at Preston, he was their Player of the Year in 2017. At Celtic he was twice Player of the Year.

Josh MAJA | 20

POSITION: Striker **NATIONALITY:** English **DOB:** 27.12.1998

PREVIOUS CLUBS: Fulham, Crystal Palace (and Man. City youth team).
INTERNATIONAL HONOURS: None, but has been called up by Nigeria.
DID YOU KNOW? Born in London, Josh made his Sunderland debut in the capital against QPR last season.

Adam MATTHEWS | 21

POSITION: Right-back **NATIONALITY:** Welsh **DOB:** 13.01.1992

PREVIOUS CLUBS: Cardiff City, Celtic and Bristol City.
INTERNATIONAL HONOURS: Wales.
DID YOU KNOW? Adam won four league titles and two cups while he was with Celtic.

Donald LOVE | 22

POSITION: Right-back **NATIONALITY:** Scottish **DOB:** 02.12.1994

PREVIOUS CLUBS: Northwich Town, Manchester United and Wigan Athletic.
INTERNATIONAL HONOURS: Scotland Under 21.
DID YOU KNOW? Donald joined Sunderland from Manchester United in a double deal with Paddy McNair.

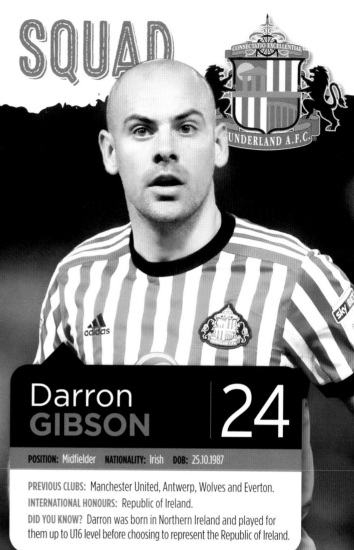

Darron GIBSON | 24

POSITION: Midfielder **NATIONALITY:** Irish **DOB:** 25.10.1987

PREVIOUS CLUBS: Manchester United, Antwerp, Wolves and Everton.
INTERNATIONAL HONOURS: Republic of Ireland.
DID YOU KNOW? Darron was born in Northern Ireland and played for them up to U16 level before choosing to represent the Republic of Ireland.

Lamine KONE | 23

POSITION: Centre-back **NATIONALITY:** French **DOB:** 01.02.1989

PREVIOUS CLUBS: SO Paris, US Alfortville, Chateauroux, Lorient & Lorient B.
INTERNATIONAL HONOURS: France Under 20. Ivory Coast.
DID YOU KNOW? When Kone scored twice against Everton in the game that kept Sunderland up in 2016 he became the first central defender to score twice in a top-flight game for Sunderland for over a century.

Robbin RUITER | 25

POSITION: Goalkeeper **NATIONALITY:** Dutch **DOB:** 25.03.1987

PREVIOUS CLUBS: FC Volendam and FC Utrecht.
INTERNATIONAL HONOURS: None.
DID YOU KNOW? Although the rebound was converted, Robbin saved a penalty on his Sunderland debut in the Carabao Cup at Carlisle.

George
HONEYMAN | 26

POSITION: Midfielder **NATIONALITY:** English **DOB:** 02.09.1994

PREVIOUS CLUBS: Gateshead.

INTERNATIONAL HONOURS: None.

DID YOU KNOW? George scored the first goal of his career in the Carabao Cup this season and followed up with his first league goal a week later.

Lynden
GOOCH | 27

POSITION: Midfielder / Forward **NATIONALITY:** American **DOB:** 24.12.1995

PREVIOUS CLUBS: Gateshead and Doncaster Rovers.

INTERNATIONAL HONOURS: USA.

DID YOU KNOW? Sunderland won 6-3 on Lynden's debut in a League Cup tie against Exeter.

Ethan
ROBSON | 28

POSITION: Midfielder **NATIONALITY:** English **DOB:** 25.10.1996

PREVIOUS CLUBS: None.

INTERNATIONAL HONOURS: None.

DID YOU KNOW? Ethan won the PL2 (Reserve League) Player of the Month award in August 2016.

Marc WILSON | 36

POSITION: Defender   **NATIONALITY:** Irish   **DOB:** 17.08.1987

PREVIOUS CLUBS: Portsmouth, Yeovil Town, Bournemouth, Luton Town, Stoke City, Bournemouth and West Bromwich Albion.

INTERNATIONAL HONOURS: Republic of Ireland.

DID YOU KNOW? Marc was a teammate of former SAFC players, Thomas Sorensen, Rory Delap, Kenwyne Jones, Dean Whitehead and Danny Collins for Stoke in the 2011 FA Cup final against Manchester City.

Joel ASORO | 29

POSITION: Striker   **NATIONALITY:** Swedish   **DOB:** 27.04.1999

PREVIOUS CLUBS: IFK Haninge and IF Brommapojkarna.

INTERNATIONAL HONOURS: Sweden Under 21.

DID YOU KNOW? Joel is the youngest Sunderland player to appear in the Premier League.

Elliot EMBLETON | 40

POSITION: Midfielder   **NATIONALITY:** English   **DOB:** 02.04.1999

PREVIOUS CLUBS: None.

INTERNATIONAL HONOURS: England Under 19.

DID YOU KNOW? Elliott helped England win the U18 Toulon Tournament last summer and was called up by U19s for the first time in August.

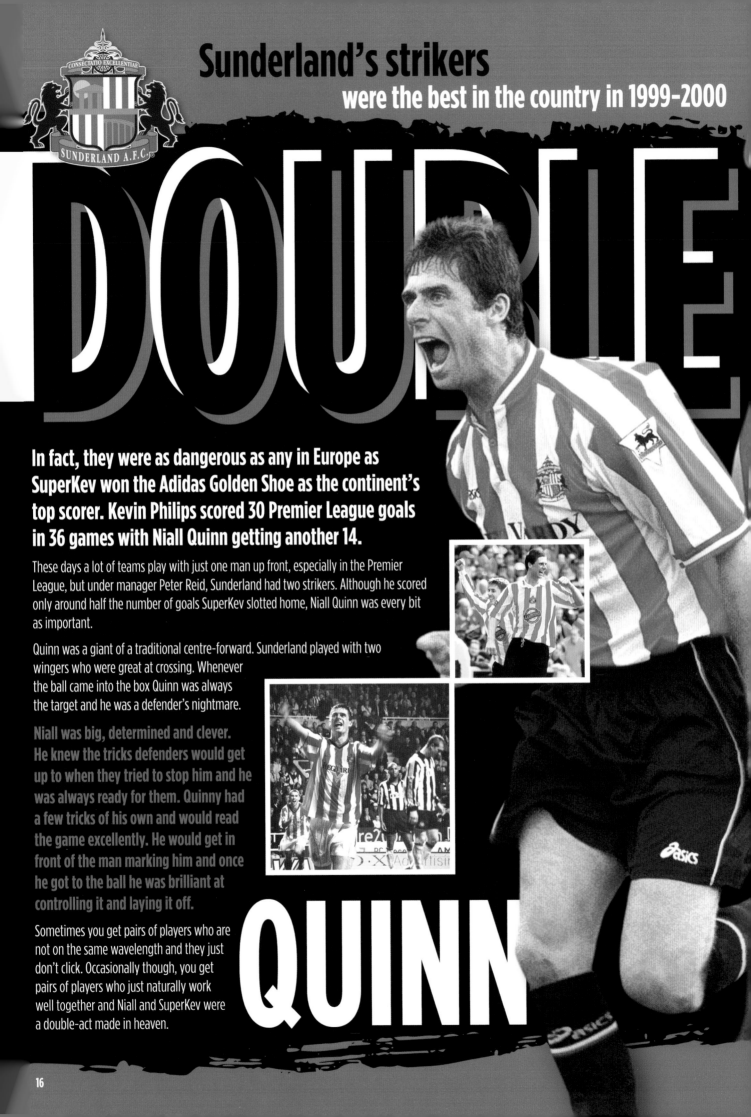

Sunderland's strikers
were the best in the country in 1999–2000

DOUBLE

In fact, they were as dangerous as any in Europe as SuperKev won the Adidas Golden Shoe as the continent's top scorer. Kevin Philips scored 30 Premier League goals in 36 games with Niall Quinn getting another 14.

These days a lot of teams play with just one man up front, especially in the Premier League, but under manager Peter Reid, Sunderland had two strikers. Although he scored only around half the number of goals SuperKev slotted home, Niall Quinn was every bit as important.

Quinn was a giant of a traditional centre-forward. Sunderland played with two wingers who were great at crossing. Whenever the ball came into the box Quinn was always the target and he was a defender's nightmare.

Niall was big, determined and clever. He knew the tricks defenders would get up to when they tried to stop him and he was always ready for them. Quinny had a few tricks of his own and would read the game excellently. He would get in front of the man marking him and once he got to the ball he was brilliant at controlling it and laying it off.

Sometimes you get pairs of players who are not on the same wavelength and they just don't click. Occasionally though, you get pairs of players who just naturally work well together and Niall and SuperKev were a double-act made in heaven.

QUINN

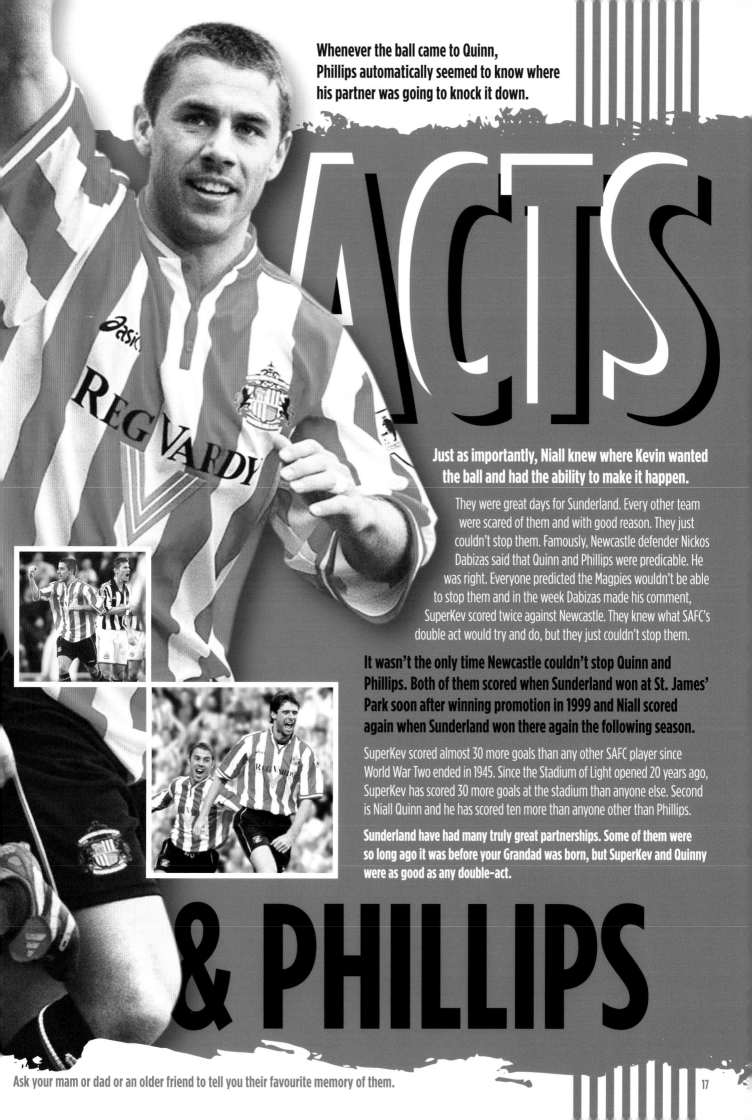

Whenever the ball came to Quinn, Phillips automatically seemed to know where his partner was going to knock it down.

ACTS

Just as importantly, Niall knew where Kevin wanted the ball and had the ability to make it happen.

They were great days for Sunderland. Every other team were scared of them and with good reason. They just couldn't stop them. Famously, Newcastle defender Nickos Dabizas said that Quinn and Phillips were predicable. He was right. Everyone predicted the Magpies wouldn't be able to stop them and in the week Dabizas made his comment, SuperKev scored twice against Newcastle. They knew what SAFC's double act would try and do, but they just couldn't stop them.

It wasn't the only time Newcastle couldn't stop Quinn and Phillips. Both of them scored when Sunderland won at St. James' Park soon after winning promotion in 1999 and Niall scored again when Sunderland won there again the following season.

SuperKev scored almost 30 more goals than any other SAFC player since World War Two ended in 1945. Since the Stadium of Light opened 20 years ago, SuperKev has scored 30 more goals at the stadium than anyone else. Second is Niall Quinn and he has scored ten more than anyone other than Phillips.

Sunderland have had many truly great partnerships. Some of them were so long ago it was before your Grandad was born, but SuperKev and Quinny were as good as any double-act.

& PHILLIPS

Ask your mam or dad or an older friend to tell you their favourite memory of them.

JAMES 9
VAUGHAN

JULIO ARCA A TRUE BLACK CAT LEGEND

1. Julio Arca was just 19 years old when he moved from his home in Argentina to sign for Sunderland in 2000. He was a very talented footballer who helped Argentina win the Under 20 World Cup at the end of his first season in English football.

2. Sunderland had just finished seventh in the Premier League and would do so again in Julio's first season. The crowd were lapping up quality football and took to this skilful, hard working young lad who had moved to the other side of the world and scored a header in his first game.

3. Sunderland enjoyed good times when Julio joined, but there were bad times too. When the club were relegated in 2003, most of the crowd's favourite players were transferred except for Arca who stayed and helped the team win promotion in 2005. His loyalty added to his already massive popularity.

4. In August 2003, the team had just ended the worst run in the club's history. Suddenly they started winning and in a game at Bradford, Arca scored one of the best goals anyone has seen Sunderland score. He ran over half the length of the pitch, dribbling around any defenders who challenged him, before beautifully chipping the ball over the City goalie.

5. After winning promotion in 2005, Sunderland started the following season very badly. When they went to Middlesbrough they were bottom of the league, but stunned Boro by winning 2-0. For the second goal, Julio floated a fabulous free-kick over the defensive wall for another classic goal by the ace Argentinian.

6. Two years later, Julio scored in another Middlesbrough v Sunderland game, but this time it was for Boro after his transfer to them. Still with Sunderland in his heart, Julio didn't celebrate. He still came to support Sunderland when he could, still lives in Sunderland now he has finished playing and coaches some of Sunderland's young players.

A JUBILANT JULIO FOLLOWING HIS STUNNING FREE-KICK AGAINST BORO

JULIO CELEBRATES HIS DEBUT GOAL AGAINST WEST HAM UNITED

JULIO'S SIX STEPS TO STARDOM

ALEX SMITHIES
QPR

Now 27, former England U19 international Alex, was at one time rated as one of the country's hottest young goalkeepers after breaking into Huddersfield's first eleven when just 17. Despite a lot of interest, he stayed with the West Yorkshire side, playing 274 games for the Terriers until his 2015 move to the capital.

KEIREN WESTWOOD
SHEFFIELD WEDNESDAY

Keiren's excellent displays between the sticks have been rewarded with over 20 international caps for the Republic of Ireland. The excellent shot-stopper has made over 130 appearances each for Sheffield Wednesday, Coventry City and Carlisle United as well as being honoured with the Player of the Year award at each club!

ADAM DAVIES
BARNSLEY

Although Adam was born in Germany, the 25-year-old comes from a Welsh family and although he's yet to debut, he has been a part of several Wales squads. After starting his career at Everton followed by a spell with Sheffield Wednesday, Davies is now a real safe pair of hands for the Tykes with over 100 appearances behind him.

goalkeepers

The value of a great goalkeeper just can't be underestimated. We've selected six top stoppers who will look to shine over the coming months.

FELIX WIEDWALD
LEEDS UNITED

After making the move to Yorkshire from Werder Bremen in the summer former Germany U20 international Felix really caught the eye and did so well that he was chosen ahead of Leeds United's ex-England 'keeper Rob Green. The imposing 6' 3" goalie has also played in Germany with MSV Duisburg and Eintracht Frankfurt.

SCOTT CARSON
DERBY COUNTY

The former England goalkeeper is still one of the best 'keepers around. Scott commands his penalty area and has a real presence on the pitch. After starting out with a handful of appearances for both Leeds United and Liverpool, Carson has now played over 400 career games in England and Turkey.

VITO MANNONE
READING

Vito came to England from Atalanta and continued his career at Arsenal. Following loan spells with Barnsley and Hull City, he went north to Sunderland where he was the hero of the Black Cats' run to the 2014 League Cup final, starring in their semi-final shoot-out win against Manchester United at Old Trafford. Player of the Year at the Stadium of Light that year, Mannone moved to the Madejski Stadium last summer.

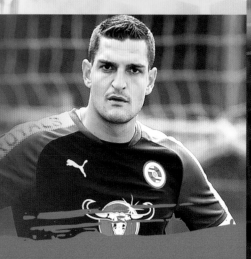

MICHAEL DAWSON
HULL CITY

Former England and Spurs centre-back, Michael made his name with Nottingham Forest before moving to the capital in 2005. The commanding defender has been voted Player of the Year with both Tottenham and the Tigers as well as winning the League Cup with Spurs a decade ago. The City skipper's consistent displays have seen him selected for the PFA Team of the Year at both ends of his career, in 2003 and 2016.

JOHN TERRY
ASTON VILLA

John is a modern-day legend. After over 700 appearances for Chelsea, and 78 for England, Terry had plenty of choices after leaving Stamford Bridge, but was convinced of Aston Villa's attractions by Steve Bruce, once a top-class centre-back himself. He has won everything going with Chelsea and has more individual awards than one trophy cabinet can hold.

RYAN SESSEGNON
FULHAM

Probably the best young player in the Championship, London-born Sessegnon is the cousin of the former Sunderland and WBA, Benin international Stephane Sessegnon. Ryan debuted for Fulham in August 2016 when he was only 16. Despite playing at left-back, he was joint top scorer at the 2017 European U19 tournament won with England.

defenders

Protecting a lead, battling for that all-important clean sheet and trying to help support their attack-minded teammates – here are six top quality Championship defenders to look out for.

SOULEYMANE BAMBA
CARDIFF CITY

Experienced Ivory Coast international centre-back Souleymane was born in France and began his playing career with Paris Saint-Germain before a move to Dunfermline. After plying his trade in Scotland, England, Turkey and Italy, Bamba made Wales the sixth country he has called home when he signed for Neil Warnock's Bluebirds.

JOHN EGAN
BRENTFORD

The Republic of Ireland international centre-back has the happy knack of chipping in with his share of goals. He is a proper centre-back, a leader with a real hunger to keep the ball out of the net. John's dad was a famous Gaelic footballer while his mother has a League of Ireland winners medal with Cork Rangers, so it's no surprise he is a talented lad destined for the top.

NATHAN BAKER
BRISTOL CITY

After 13 years and over 100 games for Aston Villa, former England U21 international left-footed centre-back Nathan Baker signed for the Robins last summer after spending the previous season on loan at Ashton Gate. Brave and committed, Villa's loss is certainly Bristol's gain.

CHEIKH NDOYE
BIRMINGHAM CITY

A commanding 6ft 3ins powerhouse in the centre of midfield, Senegal international Cheikh moved to St. Andrew's in 2017 from French club Angers who he skippered in last season's Coupe de France final, narrowly losing 1-0 to all conquering Paris Saint-Germain. He previously played for Creteil with whom he won the Championnat National (the third division of the French football) in 2013.

AIDEN McGEADY
SUNDERLAND

With almost 100 caps for the Republic of Ireland, Aiden is one of the most magical wingers in the championship. In 2010 he commanded a fee of almost £10m when joining Spartak Moscow from Celtic with whom he had won seven trophies. He arrived at the Stadium of Light from Everton after playing for Black Cats boss Simon Grayson last season on loan to Preston.

DANIEL JOHNSON
PRESTON NORTH END

Originally from Kingston, Jamaica, Daniel is unmistakable with his very long hair and equally unmistakable with the energy he shows all over the pitch. He progressed through the Aston Villa academy and went on a trio of loans before Preston signed him in January 2015. Eight goals from midfield from 23 games that season helped power Preston to promotion.

midfielders

The Championship is packed with top-class midfield performers - we've chosen six midfield maestros who could well be real star turns for their respective clubs this season.

NATHAN THOMAS
SHEFFIELD UNITED

A talented and exciting winger, Nathan made the jump from, just relegated from League two Hartlepool, to just promoted from League one Sheffield United and got off to a flying start with a debut goal in a League Cup win over Walsall. He likes to score the spectacular, finding the back of the net nine times for struggling Hartlepool last season and it's only a matter of time until Thomas is a fans' favourite at Bramall Lane.

JEM KARACAN
BOLTON WANDERERS

Jem is at his best when he's hassling and disrupting the opposition's midfield with his typically high-energy performance. London-born to an English mother and Turkish father, Jem has played for Turkey at junior levels and been in full international squads, but has yet to make his full international debut. Has played club football in Turkey as well as England and after starting over 150 games for Reading, he joined Bolton from Galatasary in 2017.

RUBEN NEVES
WOLVES

Wanderers' Portuguese international record-signing midfielder from Porto cost a reported £15.8m in 2017. Neves is just 20, but reads the game like a seasoned professional and seems destined for the top. Wolves hope this natural leader will guide them to the Premier League. Ruben is also the youngest player to captain a team in the Champions League, Porto at the age of 18.

CHAMPIONSHIP**KEY**PLAYERS

MARVIN SORDELL
BURTON ALBION

Still only 26, Marvin seems to have been around for a long time. He represented Great Britain at the 2012 London Olympics and has also played for England at U21 level. He made his name with Watford and once commanded a big money move into the Premier League with Bolton. He is a consistent and versatile performer who likes to shoot from distance.

DARYL MURPHY
NOTTINGHAM FOREST

The Republic of Ireland international was the Championship's top scorer in 2014-15 with Ipswich Town when the targetman's power and pace also earned him the Tractor Boys' Player of the Year award. He won Premier League promotion with Newcastle United last season and Sunderland in 2007 and also had a spell with Celtic in the SPL at the start of the decade.

STEVE MORISON
MILLWALL

33-year-old Steve is a Lions legend. He is now in his third spell with the club and is the reigning Millwall Player of the Year. The towering striker has scored over 230 goals in a career that started in 2001 with Northampton Town and has seen him play for England at 'C' level (non-league), before becoming a full international with Wales.

forwards

Goals win games and when it comes to finding the back of the net at Championship level, they don't come much sharper than these six great goal-getters.

BRITT ASSOMBALONGA
MIDDLESBROUGH

Britt is arguably, considered the best striker outside the Premier League. He is a proven goalscorer in the Championship, scoring 30 goals in 47 league starts for Forest. The Teessiders invested £15m to bring in the son of a former Zaire international and if he stays injury-free, could fire the boro back into the Premier League.

NELSON OLIVEIRA
NORWICH CITY

The Portugal international is a threatening striker, quick off the mark with first-class technique and neat footwork. Nelson, who started with Benfica, had six loans with clubs in Portugal, France, England and Wales, before committing his future to the Carrow Road club in 2016. He scored 15 times in 31 games in his first season as a Canary and commenced the current campaign with three goals in his first three matches.

MARTYN WAGHORN
IPSWICH TOWN

The former England U21 international returned to the English league last summer after two years in Scotland with Rangers where he won a Player of the Year award to go with the Young Player of the Year trophy he won with Leicester. Martyn has the ability to play anywhere across the front four and his good scoring record continued this season with four goals in his first three Championship games.

GOAL OF THE YEAR

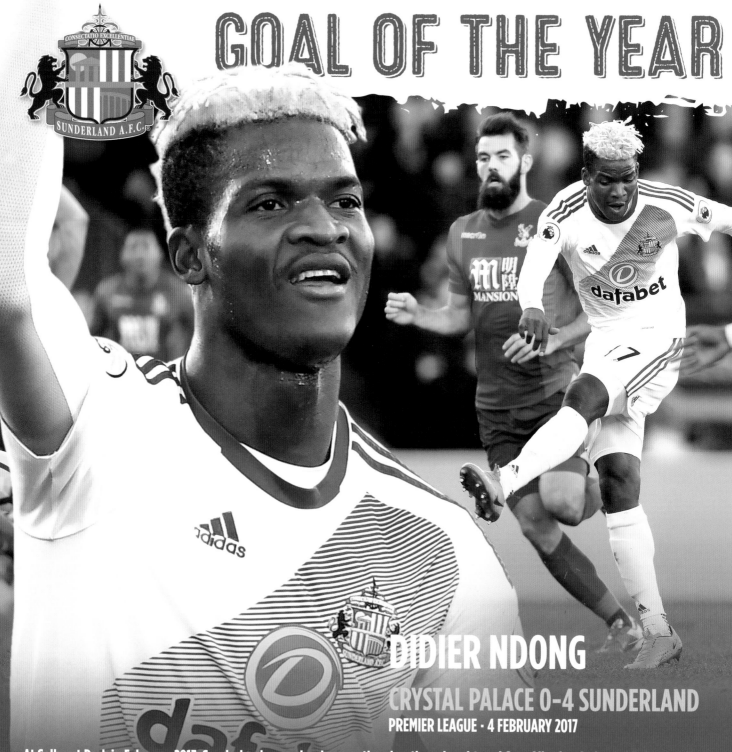

DIDIER NDONG

CRYSTAL PALACE 0-4 SUNDERLAND
PREMIER LEAGUE · 4 FEBRUARY 2017

At Selhurst Park in February 2017, Sunderland were simply sensational as they slaughtered Sam Allardyce's Crystal Palace on their own patch. It was a brilliant day and Didier Ndong's first goal for the club was an absolute peach!

There were just two minutes to go to half-time when the blonde midfielder won the ball in the centre of the park. Dispossessing Joe Ledley, Ndong burst forward, looked up and struck a superb shot from way outside the box to strengthen Sunderland's score-line. Already leading through Lamine Kone's early goal, the Black Cats had their tails up and incredibly scored twice more in first-half injury-time through Jermain Defoe. Four up at the interval Sunderland showed a disciplined approach after the break, denying Palace any route back into the game as Jordan Pickford kept a clean sheet.

It was the first time Palace had ever conceded four goals in the first half of a Premier League fixture and the result meant that Jack Rodwell's long record of Premier League starts for Sunderland without being on the winning side thankfully came to an end.

Ndong, from Gabon in West Africa has shown himself to be a hard working player, full of energy and determination. Just 22 years of age at the time, the goal was only the sixth of Ndong's career, but it was one he deserved. His goal and the result were fantastic!

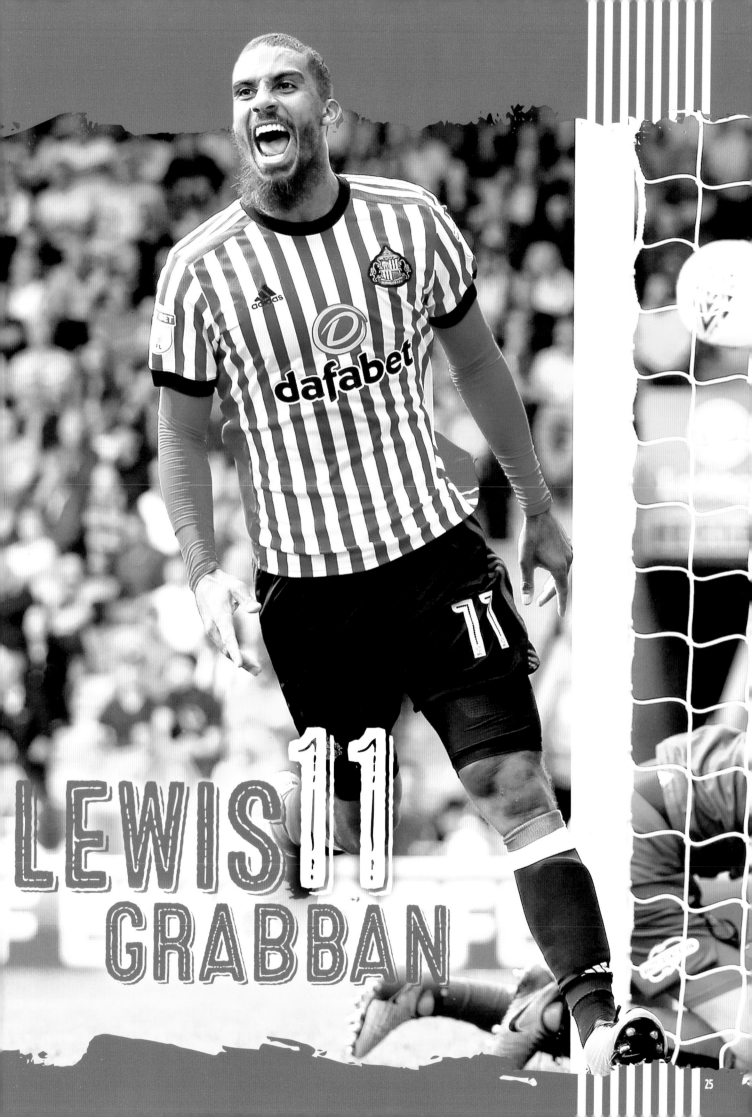

LEWIS **11**
GRABBAN

WHO ARE YER

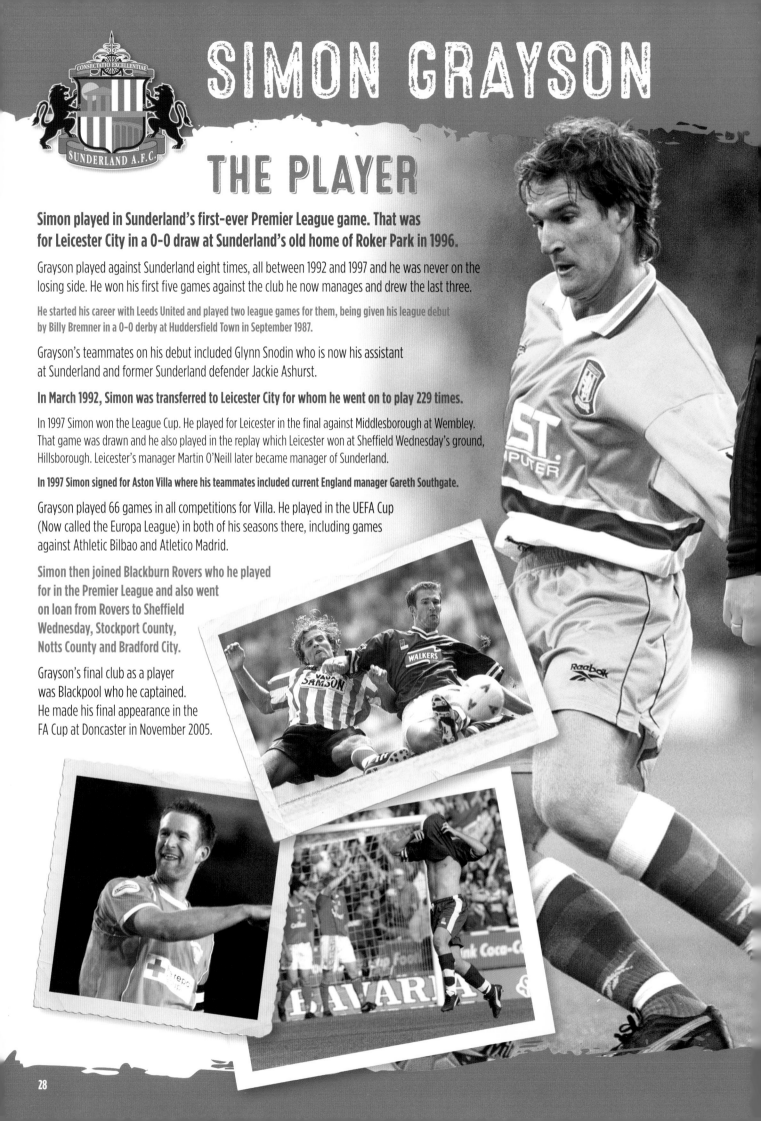

SIMON GRAYSON

THE PLAYER

Simon played in Sunderland's first-ever Premier League game. That was for Leicester City in a 0-0 draw at Sunderland's old home of Roker Park in 1996.

Grayson played against Sunderland eight times, all between 1992 and 1997 and he was never on the losing side. He won his first five games against the club he now manages and drew the last three.

He started his career with Leeds United and played two league games for them, being given his league debut by Billy Bremner in a 0-0 derby at Huddersfield Town in September 1987.

Grayson's teammates on his debut included Glynn Snodin who is now his assistant at Sunderland and former Sunderland defender Jackie Ashurst.

In March 1992, Simon was transferred to Leicester City for whom he went on to play 229 times.

In 1997 Simon won the League Cup. He played for Leicester in the final against Middlesborough at Wembley. That game was drawn and he also played in the replay which Leicester won at Sheffield Wednesday's ground, Hillsborough. Leicester's manager Martin O'Neill later became manager of Sunderland.

In 1997 Simon signed for Aston Villa where his teammates included current England manager Gareth Southgate.

Grayson played 66 games in all competitions for Villa. He played in the UEFA Cup (Now called the Europa League) in both of his seasons there, including games against Athletic Bilbao and Atletico Madrid.

Simon then joined Blackburn Rovers who he played for in the Premier League and also went on loan from Rovers to Sheffield Wednesday, Stockport County, Notts County and Bradford City.

Grayson's final club as a player was Blackpool who he captained. He made his final appearance in the FA Cup at Doncaster in November 2005.

Simon Grayson is Sunderland's manager.

He has won promotion four times as a manager and hopefully that will become five times while he is in charge at the Stadium of Light.

THE MANAGER

Simon Grayson has won promotion to the championship with Blackpool, Leeds United, Huddersfield Town and Preston North End.

He won the Manager of the Month Award three times with Preston, once with Leeds and twice with Blackpool.

Simon began his managerial career with the club where he finished his playing career: Blackpool. Having been a coach at the club from 2004-05, Simon took over as manager on 24 November 2005, the same month he played his final match.

Grayson grabbed promotion in his first full season with Blackpool, beating Yeovil in the Play-Off final in 2007 as Blackpool rocked up a club record 10th win in a row.

In December 2008, Simon took over as manager of Leeds United and in that first season took them into the Play-Offs where they went down to Millwall.

Simon saw his Leeds United team pull off a famous cup win away to Manchester United in 2008-09 and won automatic promotion a season later.

Newly promoted Leeds did well to finish seventh in their first season back in the Championship, but by the start of February 2012, he parted ways with the Yorkshire club after three years and two months at Elland Road.

Within three weeks Leeds United near neighbours Huddersfield Town stepped in to appoint Simon as replacement for former Sunderland player Lee Clark.

Huddersfield Town won immediate promotion under Simon, beating Sheffield United in the Play-off final.

In 2013, Simon became manager of Preston North End. He reached the Play-offs in his first full season, losing to Rotherham, before winning promotion a year later after beating Swindon Town in the Play-Offs. He remained PNE boss until Sunderland came in for him in the summer of 2017.

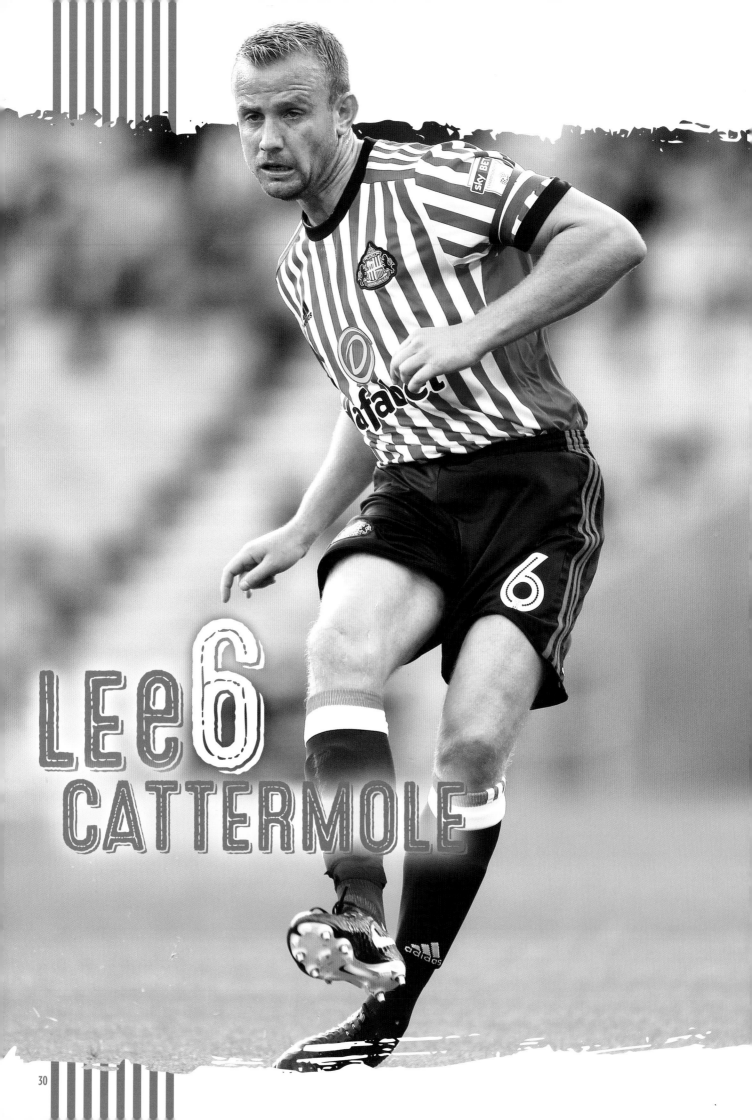

LEE 6
CATTERMOLE

FOOTBALL 50

```
S U B S T I T U T E I S R E D L E I F D I M
M A A Z P L E A O S U J J Y O Y T N D T R K O
A Q E X T R A T I M E R L C K J A U D I M E
N B L C A C A D E M Y K F Y U K O B C B N P
O N I E S A J W R T P E X R T G D K H B P B
F R F J A P H I A E M R Y C U C O C A L T L
T H I W Y T D B K W S T O D Y F B R L I E I
H D N E P A R X J B I S C M F A U O L N E T
E D A Z L I N E S M A N I T O F D G E G H R
M B L D S N W A E C Q I U N A T P U N Q S A
A I W Y H C O R N E R F L A G O I M G Z N N
T E H E A D E R V L H Y S R I R C O E R A S
C B I M J E E L U R E D I S F F O K N V E F
H G S G Q F P R N U A L K L G I H O B M L E
F R T U F E L N B T F E R E G A N A M A C R
M E L K E N G F B Y D H T D A F V G O H J W
Y K E F C D R P O C M F H L H J W G A B H I
S I O W O E K S P U I A O A V S N F D M I N
A R W M N R Q N R P L H T U O E M S R T J D
O T K C I K E E R F Y T D C D J Y B A G T O
G S O V T C A D T B R X N L H S F A C U P W
K A M P Q E T I C I E F O M R N G E W B S U
C I A M S K M R C A S G C G O U K O O C E M
I Y E J A E R K D I R F H S R E Y A L P V C
K C T E P D R G B F K D A E U G A E L E R S
R E T L T N W T J N G E Q U A L I S E R E H
O Y S P A I A W N G S R C V S F G L Y F S R
S S R N T N H L H E L S U N U T M E G U E N
S K I J S J E V R L C W A S P O L S O F R J
I K F P F H M P L K U F E H E L A O E T I M
C R O S S B A R S C T T M R O J I R W T Q N
S O I R M E X I C A N W A V E P E O L D K P
G A S U N N A E R T U B R E P E E K L A O G
```

Academy
Captain
Centre Spot
Challenge
Clean Sheet
Corner Flag
Crossbar
Defender
Derby Match
Dressing Room
Dribbling
Dugout
Equaliser
Extra Time
FA Cup
Fans
Final Whistle
First Team
Fixture
Foul
Free Kick
Goalkeeper
Golden Goal
Half Time
Hat-trick
Header
Injury Time
Kick-off
League
Linesman
Manager
Man of the Match
Mexican Wave
Midfielder
Nutmeg
Offside Rule
Penalty
Players
Pre-season
Promotion
Red Card
Referee
Reserves
Scissor Kick
Striker
Substitute
Tackle
Transfer Window
Volley
Yellow Card

Gabbiadini and Gates were known as the 'G-Force'

DOUBLE

Eric Gates was an experienced England international coming to the end of his career. Marco Gabbiadini was a young, fast and powerful striker. Their double-act devastated opponents.

Sunderland simply got the ball to Gates, he put it in front of Gabbiadini and defences watched as Marco left them in his wake as he stormed through to score. Simple but superb!

The moment that summed up the G-Force came in one of the most important derby matches ever. The year was 1990 and Sunderland met Newcastle in the Play-Offs. Can you imagine that? A derby match is amazing at any time, but a derby match in the Play-Offs is just incredible.

The first leg had finished 0-0 at Sunderland where the red and whites had missed a penalty won by Marco. At Newcastle though, Gates put Sunderland one up early on and as the game neared its end, 'Gatesy' slipped a ball into Gabbiadini's path. Marco did what he did so often and finished it off. Newcastle fans invaded the pitch to try and get the match abandoned but they failed. They had been blown away by the G-Force.

GABBIADINI

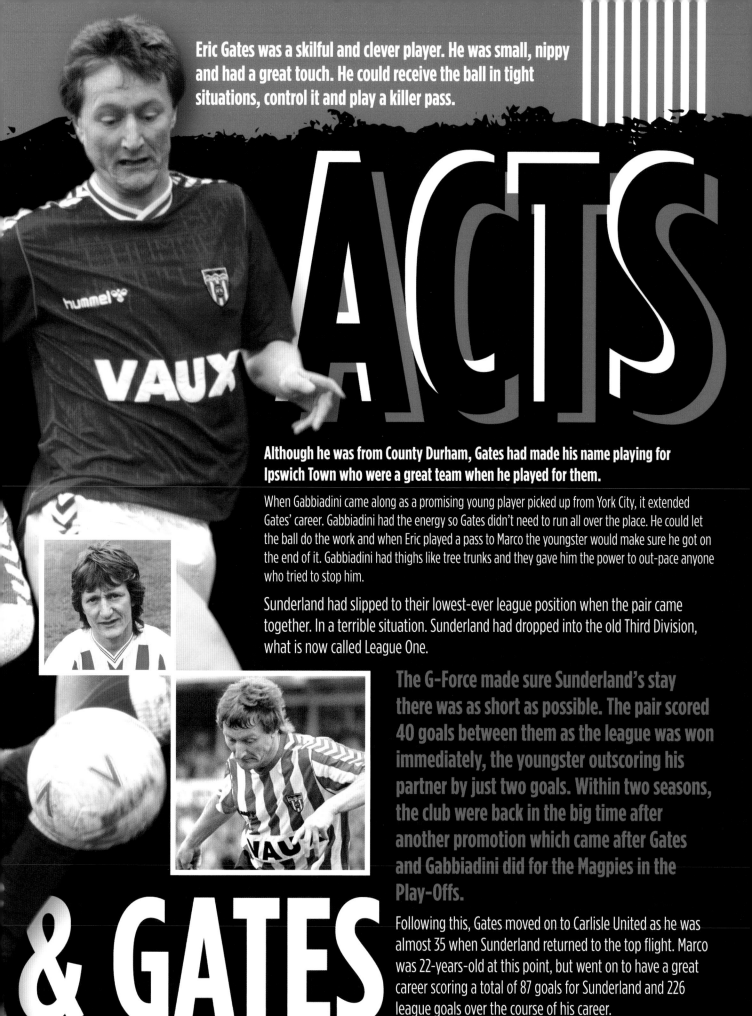

Eric Gates was a skilful and clever player. He was small, nippy and had a great touch. He could receive the ball in tight situations, control it and play a killer pass.

ACTS

Although he was from County Durham, Gates had made his name playing for Ipswich Town who were a great team when he played for them.

When Gabbiadini came along as a promising young player picked up from York City, it extended Gates' career. Gabbiadini had the energy so Gates didn't need to run all over the place. He could let the ball do the work and when Eric played a pass to Marco the youngster would make sure he got on the end of it. Gabbiadini had thighs like tree trunks and they gave him the power to out-pace anyone who tried to stop him.

Sunderland had slipped to their lowest-ever league position when the pair came together. In a terrible situation. Sunderland had dropped into the old Third Division, what is now called League One.

The G-Force made sure Sunderland's stay there was as short as possible. The pair scored 40 goals between them as the league was won immediately, the youngster outscoring his partner by just two goals. Within two seasons, the club were back in the big time after another promotion which came after Gates and Gabbiadini did for the Magpies in the Play-Offs.

Following this, Gates moved on to Carlisle United as he was almost 35 when Sunderland returned to the top flight. Marco was 22-years-old at this point, but went on to have a great career scoring a total of 87 goals for Sunderland and 226 league goals over the course of his career.

& GATES

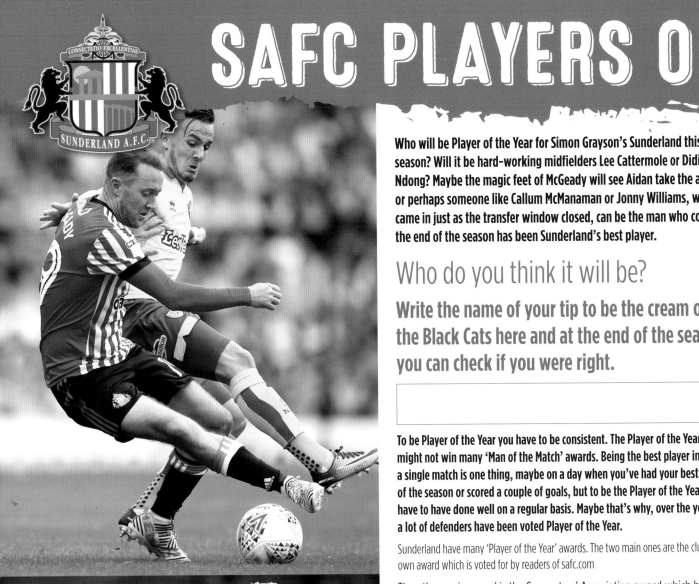

SAFC PLAYERS OF

Who will be Player of the Year for Simon Grayson's Sunderland this season? Will it be hard-working midfielders Lee Cattermole or Didier Ndong? Maybe the magic feet of McGeady will see Aidan take the award or perhaps someone like Callum McManaman or Jonny Williams, who came in just as the transfer window closed, can be the man who come the end of the season has been Sunderland's best player.

Who do you think it will be?

Write the name of your tip to be the cream of the Black Cats here and at the end of the season you can check if you were right.

To be Player of the Year you have to be consistent. The Player of the Year might not win many 'Man of the Match' awards. Being the best player in a single match is one thing, maybe on a day when you've had your best game of the season or scored a couple of goals, but to be the Player of the Year you have to have done well on a regular basis. Maybe that's why, over the years, a lot of defenders have been voted Player of the Year.

Sunderland have many 'Player of the Year' awards. The two main ones are the club's own award which is voted for by readers of safc.com

The other main award is the Supporters' Association award which has been going for more years than the club's own award. Many individual branches of the Supporters' Association also have their own individual award which is how Bobby Moncur - who captained Sunderland in the mid-seventies - won an award before the main awards started!

The first time the overall Supporters' Association made a Player of the Year award was in 1976-77 when left-back Joe Bolton was the winner. The club started their own award, run through the club programme and Sunderland Echo in those days in 1980-81. Usually the same player wins both awards, but not every time. Forward Stan Cummins won the first club Player of the Year award and doubled-up with the Supporters' Association award, but, for instance, modern day club ambassador Kevin Ball won the official award just once in 1990-91 (his first season with the club), but won the Fans' trophy four times.

Bally won both awards in 1990-91 and went on to also be Supporters' Association Player of the Year in 1992-93, 1994-95 and 1996-97. In those seasons the club's official award went to striker Don Goodman, right-back Dariusz Kubicki and goalkeeper Lionel Perez.

Strikers Marco Gabbiadini and Jermain Defoe are the only men to win the official award two years running. Defoe won it in the two most recent seasons while Gabbiadini took it in 1988-89 and 1989-90.

Super Kevin Phillips won the award in 1997-98 and 1999-00 with his front partner Niall Quinn the winner in the season in between.

Defender Gary Bennett, who you still hear summarising matches on the radio, was Player of the Year in 1986-87 and 1993-94. No-one else has won the award so many years apart.

THE YEAR

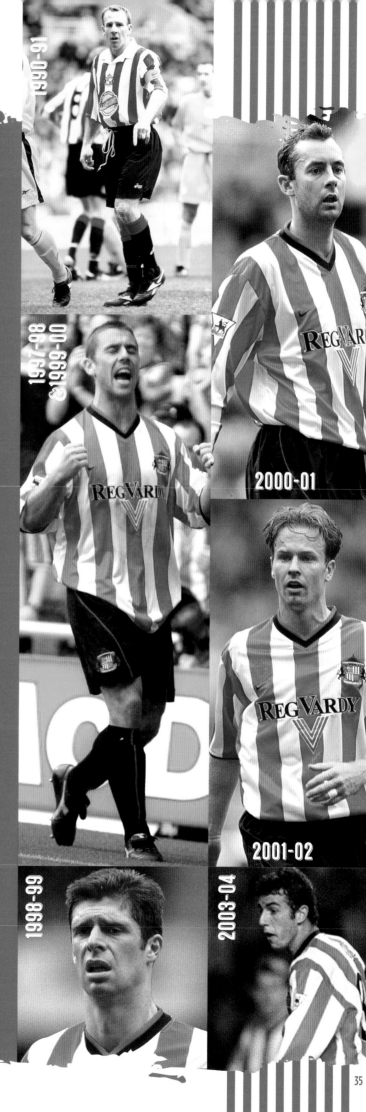

PLAYER OF THE YEAR OFFICIAL CLUB AWARD

1980-81	Stan Cummins
1981-82	Nick Pickering
1982-83	Ian Atkins
1983-84	Paul Bracewell
1984-85	Chris Turner
1985-86	Mark Proctor
1986-87	Gary Bennett
1987-88	Eric Gates
1988-89	Marco Gabbiadini
1989-90	Marco Gabbiadini
1990-91	Kevin Ball
1991-92	John Byrne
1992-93	Don Goodman
1993-94	Gary Bennett
1994-95	Dariusz Kubicki
1995-96	Richard Ord
1996-97	Lionel Perez
1997-98	Kevin Phillips
1998-99	Niall Quinn
1999-00	Kevin Phillips
2000-01	Don Hutchison
2001-02	Jody Craddock
2002-03	Sean Thornton
2003-04	Julio Arca
2004-05	George McCartney
2005-06	Dean Whitehead
2006-07	Nyron Nosworthy
2007-08	Kenwyne Jones
2008-09	Danny Collins
2009-10	Darren Bent
2010-11	Phil Bardsley
2011-12	Stephane Sessegnon
2012-13	Simon Mignolet
2013-14	Vito Mannone
2014-15	Seb Larsson
2015-16	Jermain Defoe
2016-17	Jermaine Defoe

1990-91

1997-98 & 1999-00

2000-01

2001-02

2003-04

1998-99

1980-81

1986-87 & 1993-94

1998-99 & 1989-90

1. Born in 1981, John played for teams called Ferrybank and Waterford Bohemians in Ireland before joining Manchester United. He made his debut when he was 18 before going out on loan to gain experience with Bournemouth, who were then in what we now call League One, and Royal Antwerp in Belgium.

2. After a handful of club appearances, John made his full international debut for the Republic of Ireland when he was picked by Mick McCarthy, who later became manager of Sunderland. O'Shea has gone on to become a legend of Irish football. He scored his first goal in 2003, captained Ireland for the first time on his 80th appearance in 2012 and marked his 100th cap with his third international goal to claim a late equaliser away to World Champions Germany.

3. John started to play regularly for Manchester United in 2002-03 when he won the first of FIVE Premier League winners' medals. One of the things John became famous for was his ability to play in many different positions. In 2007, he even went in goal in a Premier League game away to Spurs!

4. John made the last of his 393 appearances for Manchester United in 2011. As well as his five Premier League medals, John also won the Champions League, World Club Cup, FA Cup, the League Cup three times and the Community Shield four times. He also played against Barcelona in the 2009 Champions League final.

5. John joined Sunderland in 2011. He has gone on to play over 200 times for the club who he captained at Wembley in the 2014 Capital One Cup final against Manchester City. At Sunderland, he has played some games at right-back and a handful as a defensive-midfielder, but mainly he has played as a centre-back.

6. Now 36, John is captain at Sunderland and vice-captain of the Republic of Ireland who he will hope to play for at next summer's FIFA World Cup if his country have qualified. John has over 100 caps for Ireland, but in a massively successful career, has never played at a World Cup.

O'SHEA'S
SIX STEPS TO STARDOM

LAMINE
23 KONE

ASTON VILLA

Which England and Chelsea legend did Aston Villa sign at the start of this season?

1 answer

Aston Villa won the European Cup in 1981. Did they beat Bayern Munich, Barcelona or Real Madrid in the final?

2 answer

Who is the former Sunderland manager who started the season as Villa manager?

3 answer

BARNSLEY

During the summer Barnsley signed Ezekiel Fryers from which Premier League London club?

5 answer

Who is Barnsley's captain?

4 answer

Who is the Tykes' manager?

6 answer

BIRMINGHAM CITY

When did Birmingham City last win the League Cup?

8 answer

Who scored Blues first league goal this season?

7 answer

City completed a record signing on transfer deadline day, summer 2017, who was it?

9 answer

BOLTON WANDERERS

How many times have Bolton won the FA Cup?

10 answer

Bolton reached the League Cup final in 2004 but lost to which club who are also now in the Championship?

11 answer

Name the manager who led Bolton to promotion in 2017 in his first season at the club.

12 answer

BRENTFORD

Brentford are West London rivals of QPR who they knocked out of this season's Carabao Cup away from home. Did they win 3-1, 4-1 or 5-1?

13 answer

Who is Brentford's Number 9 striker this season?

14 answer

Who was the manager of Brentford from 2013 to 2015 who went on to manage Rangers and Nottingham Forest?

15 answer

BRISTOL CITY

Which Premier League team did City knock out of the Carabao Cup away from home in the second round this season?

17

Who was Bristol City's Player of the Season in 2016-17?

16 answer

Which Wales international was on loan from Sunderland to Bristol City last season?

18 answer

CHALLENGE

BURTON ALBION

Who was Burton's first summer signing ahead of the 2017-18 season?

20

Which former England international began the season as Burton's manager?

19

Which former Liverpool and Villa player signed for Burton at the start of the season?

21

CARDIFF CITY

Cardiff City are the Bluebirds but what colour were their shirts between 2012 and 2015?

22

Who was the manager who inspired Cardiff to maximum points from their first four league games of this season?

23

Who was the Chile international midfielder who moved from Cardiff to Inter Milan in 2014 and stayed with the Italian giants until 2017?

24

DERBY COUNTY

Which Derby player scored the opening goal at the Stadium of Light this season?

25

In what year did Derby win the FA Cup?

26

Who is the former England international Derby re-signed for a second spell at the club at the start of this season?

27

FULHAM

Who is Fulham's No 1 this season?

29

Which Spanish side beat Fulham in the final of the 2010 Europa League?

28

Who is Fulham's No 10 and their captain this season?

30

HULL CITY

Which country did Leonid Slutsky manage before taking over at Hull?

32

What is Hull's nickname?

31

Hull reached the FA Cup final in 2014 but lost to which London club?

33

IPSWICH TOWN

Who scored Town's first league goal this season?

34

Ipswich went from the third division to top flight champions in six years under the manager who later won the World Cup for England. Who was that?

35

In which season did the Tractor Boys win the FA Cup?

36

LEEDS UNITED

What is Leeds United's club anthem?

37

Between 1965 and 1974 how many times did Leeds finish in the top two of the league?

38

Who is captaining the Whites this season?

39

MIDDLESBROUGH

Which Spanish team beat Middlesbrough in the 2006 Europa League final?

41 answer

Who did Boro sign on a season-long loan from Swansea City in July 2017?

40

Which major trophy did Boro win in 2004?

42

MILLWALL

Who did Millwall play in the 2004 FA Cup final?

44

Millwall began this season with one of their former Players of the Year as manager. Who?

43

What is Millwall's nickname?

45

NORWICH CITY

Which team did Head Coach, Daniel Farke, manage before joining City this season?

46

How many League Cup finals have Norwich played in, two, three or four?

47

Who is the Canaries No 1 this season?

48

NOTTINGHAM FOREST

Which Premier League club did Forest defeat away from home in the Carabao Cup in August 2017?

49 answer

Forest have twice won the European Cup (now the Champions League). True or false?

50

Who is the former Brighton, Leeds and Sunderland midfielder Forest signed in August 2017?

51

PRESTON NORTH END

Who was the future Everton and Manchester United manager who won the Division Two title with Preston in 2000?

53 answer

Who was Preston's top scorer last season?

52

Preston did it first in 1996, Wolves equalled it in 1988 and Burnley, Sheffield United and Portsmouth have done it since. What is the feat these five clubs have achieved?

54

CHALLENGE

QUEENS PARK RANGERS

Which defender did Rangers pay a club record £12.5m for in 2013 only to sell him later that year?

56 answer

Who is QPR's captain this season?

55 answer

Which of the following managers have not managed QPR: Harry Redknapp, Mark Hughes, Martin O'Neill and Ian Holloway?

57 answer

READING

Which former Manchester United defender was manager of Reading at the start of the season?

58 answer

What position in the Championship did Reading finish in last season?

59 answer

Who did Reading sign from Sunderland during the summer?

60 answer

SHEFFIELD UNITED

Who is the Blades' No 9 striker this season?

61 answer

How many points did Sheffield United earn in winning League One last season: 95, 100 or 105?

62 answer

Goalkeeper Jamal Blackman is on a season long loan to Sheffield United from which Premier League London club?

63 answer

SHEFFIELD WEDNESDAY

Sheffield Wednesday are one of the oldest clubs in the world. In 2017 they celebrated a major anniversary. How many years old were the club in 2017?

65 answer

Who was Sheffield Wednesday's first 2017 summer signing?

64 answer

Adding together Sheffield Wednesday's top flight league titles, FA Cup and League Cup wins, how many major trophies have they won: 6, 7 or 8?

66 answer

SUNDERLAND

How many other current Championship clubs have Sunderland met in FA Cup finals?

68 answer

Who did Sunderland sign from West Brom on August 2017 transfer deadline day ?

67 answer

Which two academy produced players scored their first goals for the club in August 2017?

69 answer

WOLVERHAMPTON WANDERERS

Who were last season's League Cup finalists who Wolves knocked out of this season's Carabao Cup in August?

70 answer

Between 1950 and 1960 how many times did Wolves finish in the top two of the top flight?

71 answer

Who is the Portuguese midfielder Wolves paid almost £16m in the summer of 2017?

72 answer

KEVIN BALL CELEBRATING
WINNING THE CHAMPIONSHIP
IN 1999

1. Signed from Portsmouth, Kevin made his debut in the first home game after promotion. The opponents were Spurs. It was straight after the 1990 World Cup when Tottenham's Gary Lineker and Paul Gascoigne were two of the top stars when England reached the semi-final. Bally was brilliant and never looked back.

2. Kevin came as a centre-back and was a very good one. He was a very tough tackler who sometimes got sent-off. but the fans could see the passion he played with. In every game he played, Bally was very determined. Fans would chant 'Ooh, Bally Bally' whenever he crunched someone in a tackle.

3. Kevin played in the 1992 FA Cup final. Sunderland were in the same division they are now, but Bally helped the Lads beat top-flight West Ham, Chelsea and Norwich City to reach Wembley. Although Liverpool won the final, Kevin and Co had done well to become the only Sunderland team to get to the final since the cup was won in 1973.

4. Kevin became captain the season after playing in the final and proved to be one of the best skippers the club have ever had. He was like a manager on the pitch, organising everyone, driving the team on and leading by example. In 1995-96 Kevin captained the team to the Championship title and promotion.

5. In 1998-99 Bally led his team to the title once again, but this time with a record 105 points. The league was already won when the final game came around, but with Sunderland losing at half-time, Kevin demanded more and more from his teammates as he didn't want to lift the trophy at the final whistle having just lost. Such commitment summed Kevin up.

6. In 1999 Kevin had a Testimonial Match against the Italian team Sampdoria at the Stadium of Light. After finishing his career with Fulham and Burnley, Bally came back to bring through young players such as Jordan Henderson who went on to captain England. Kevin later had two spells as caretaker manager. He still works at the club.

BALLY'S
SIX STEPS TO STARDOM

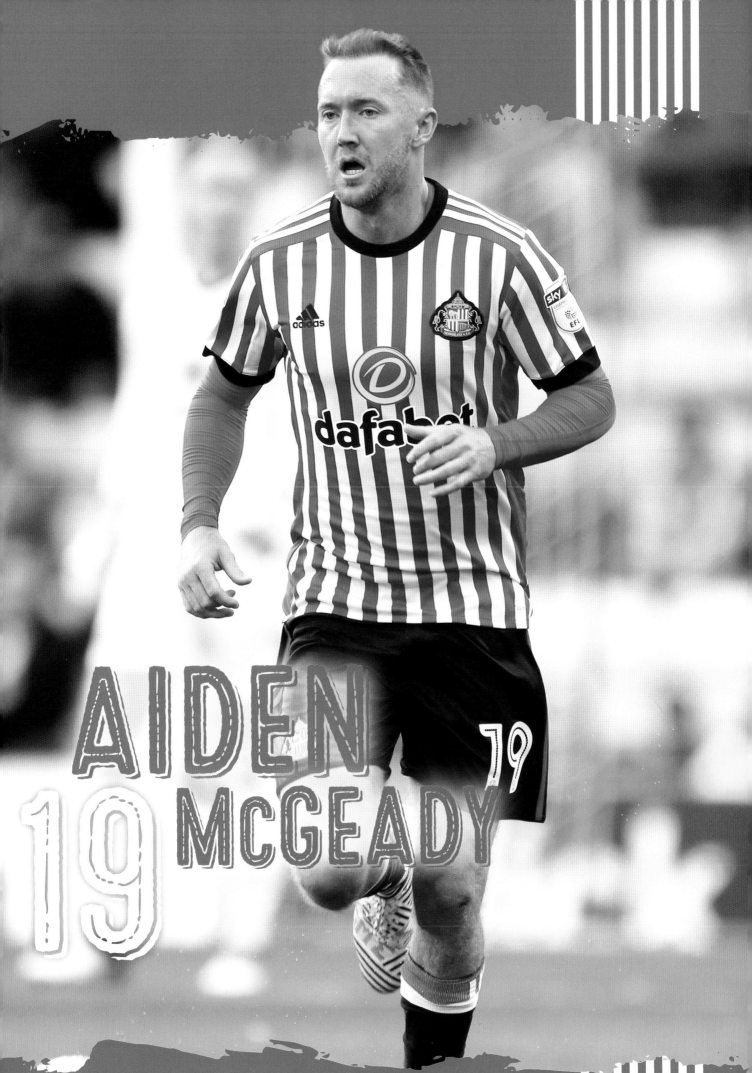

AIDEN
19 McGEADY

WORLD CUP

WHEN THE SEASON COMES TO AN END IN MAY, THE FOOTBALL DOESN'T STOP!

When Sunderland's campaign is over and the Championship prizes are handed out, you can sit back and get ready to watch the World's international super-stars take to the pitch for the 2018 FIFA World Cup which starts on 14 June.

Just to get you in the mood, ask an adult to help you try this quiz!

1930

The first World Cup was won by the host nation Uruguay, but who did they defeat 4-2 in the Final?

1950

During England's first-ever World Cup in Brazil, they were beaten 1-0 by a team of part-timers from which Country?

1966

Sunderland's mascot is Samson the Cat, but what was the official World Cup mascot called when England beat Germany 4-2 to win the World Cup?

1934

The host nation were victorious again! Italy beat Czechoslovakia 2-1, but do you know how many times the Italians have won the World Cup?

1954

Which country scored 27 goals, the most of the tournament? Ferenc Puskás netted four!

1970

Arguably the greatest World Cup final of all time was in 1970, when brilliant Brazil won 4-1. Who did they beat?

1938

Italy retained the trophy with a 4-2 victory over Hungary, in which European capital?

1958 & 1962

The same name went on the trophy in 1958 and 1962, the first and second of their record five wins. Who are they?

1974

The Dutch captain produced one of the World Cup's most iconic moments - a 180 degree wrong-footing turn that totally outwitted the defender. What is the move called?

QUIZ...

1978
Who was the Golden Boot winner with six goals, including two in the final?

1994
The record for most goals in a single match by one player is five, scored by Oleg Salenko as Cameroon were crushed 6-1 by which nation?

2006
One match, nicknamed 'the Battle of Nuremberg' ended nine-a-side as 16 yellow cards and four red cards were handed out. Who were the teams and what was the result?

1982
Which Northern Ireland player became the youngest-ever, at 17 years, one month and ten days old, to appear in the final stages of the World Cup?

1998
Who won the Golden Ball award for the tournament's best player?

2010
When England drew 1-1 with USA, which member of the USA's starting line-up went on to play for Sunderland?

1986
Which legendary Argentinian scored twice to knock England out at the quarter-final stage 2-1?

2002
This German star scored a hat-trick in the 8-0 demolition of Saudi Arabia - the first of his record 16 goals in World Cup finals. Who is he?

2014
Which product of Sunderland's Academy of Light played for England at the last World Cup?

1990
In the opening match, the holders Argentina suffered a shock 1-0 defeat by which African nation?

2018
Where are the World Cup finals going to be held next summer?

45

Most famous footballing double-acts are strike partnerships, but take a look at the defending duo of Elliott and Clarke!

DOUBLE

After all it is the goal-scorers who hog the headlines. So think how good a double-act of defenders would have to be to be anywhere near as popular as a pair of players who kept hitting the back of the net.

Jeff Clarke and Shaun Elliott were a pair of central defenders who complemented each other perfectly. They played together many years ago, their best season being in 1979-80 when they helped Sunderland to win promotion. Clarke was a big stopper centre half. He was excellent in the air and was strong enough to handle the biggest, toughest target men.

Alongside Clarke was Shaun Elliott. His greatest assets were speed combined with his ability to read the game. When a ball came into the Sunderland penalty area usually Clarke would go up to win it with Elliott covering. Most of the time Clarke would win the header but if he didn't Elliott was there to cover him, and his pace meant he was very difficult to beat.

Both Clarke and Elliott were excellent defenders, but neither of them would be Sunderland's best ever centre half. That would be either Charlie Hurley or Dave Watson or even Charlie Thompson who played over 100 years ago. However as far as central defensive partnerships go Clarke and Elliott were as good as any.

ELLIOTT

Unluckily Clarke was carried off with a very bad injury just before promotion was won in 1980. He came back and did well later in his career but had he not suffered his injury he may well have been capped by England.

FACTS & CLARKE

Elliott won three 'B' caps for England, one of them against Spain at Sunderland.

Elliott too would be troubled by injury later in his career. He should have been Sunderland's skipper at Wembley in the 1985 League Cup final but missed out through suspension.

While Elliott missed one cup final, Clarke came to the club as part of a deal that took a hero from the previous cup final away from Sunderland.

Clarke was a 21 year old up and coming defender when he left Manchester City to come to Sunderland as part exchange for Dave Watson who had been Man of the Match when Sunderland won the FA Cup in 1973. Losing Watson was a big blow but in Jeff Clarke Sunderland signed another tremendous defender and he got even better once paired up with Elliott.

Elliott was a youth teamer when Clarke arrived. It wasn't until 18 months after Clarke's arrival that Elliott broke into the team and as Jeff soon got injured and Shaun often played in midfield anyway at that time it wasn't really until 1978-79 that their partnership was given a chance to flourish, but when it did it blossomed into one of the best defensive duos you could ever wish to see.

Design their kit,
add hair, be creative!

MAKE YOUR OWN
FOOZBALL
Team

BILLY 2
JONES

CHARLIE BUCHAN

BOBBY BEST

Do you know football used to be played on Christmas Day?

Sunderland haven't done so for over 60 years, but Boxing Day games are still very popular.

25 DECEMBER 1914
NEWCASTLE UNITED 2-5 SUNDERLAND

The best player was definitely Bobby Best. He scored a hat-trick on a day when he was better than anyone else at keeping his feet on a very slippy pitch. A week earlier he had scored twice as Sunderland won 6-0 away to Spurs. Big away wins were something supporters enjoyed a lot of back then. When Sunderland won this game 5-2 it was only six years since they had beaten Newcastle by a record score of 1-9 at Newcastle!

This time they must have felt sorry for ruining The Magpies' Christmas as after getting into a 5-0 lead with 20 minutes to go Sunderland scored two own goals for Newcastle who earlier on had missed a penalty.

Sunderland had been 1-0 up when Frank Hudspeth missed his spot-kick. Having opened the scoring after just eight minutes, Best made it 2-0 just after the half hour and completed his hat-trick four minutes into the second half. That made it 4-0 as the famous Charlie Buchan had got in on the act a minute before half time. George Phillip made it five before goalkeeper Leslie Scott punched a corner into his own net and soon afterwards was beaten by a 20 yard back-pass from full-back Harry Ness.

CHRISTMAS

25 DECEMBER 1950
SUNDERLAND 2-1 MANCHESTER UTD
26 DECEMBER 1950
MANCHESTER UNITED 3-5 SUNDERLAND

Sunderland beat Manchester United twice in two days. Two goals by Tommy Wright provided a home win on Christmas Day before a hat-trick by Ivor Broadis destroyed United on their home ground a day later.

Back in those days pitches often weren't as good as they are now, especially in the winter. The icy Old Trafford surface was described as being like a skating rink. Anyone who turned up a few minutes late would have missed two goals but there were plenty more to come. The home side actually took the lead after just two minutes through John Aston, but Sunderland equalised a minute later through Billy Bingham. England international Ivor Broadis scored twice in two minutes as the half hour ticked by and completed his hat-trick two minutes before half time, United having scored through Tommy Bogan in between Broadis' second and third goals.

Brilliant Broadis back-heeled a ball to set up Dickie Davis who made it 2-5 to Sunderland in the 63rd minute and it finished 3-5 with Bogan's second goal of the game after Sunderland goalie Johnny Mapson had saved a penalty by Jack Rowley.

TOMMY WRIGHT

IVOR BROADIS

Crowds at Boxing Day games are often amongst the highest of the season!
Some of the crowd are supporters who no longer live in the North East, but are home for the holidays and want to see the Lads live at the Stadium of Light.

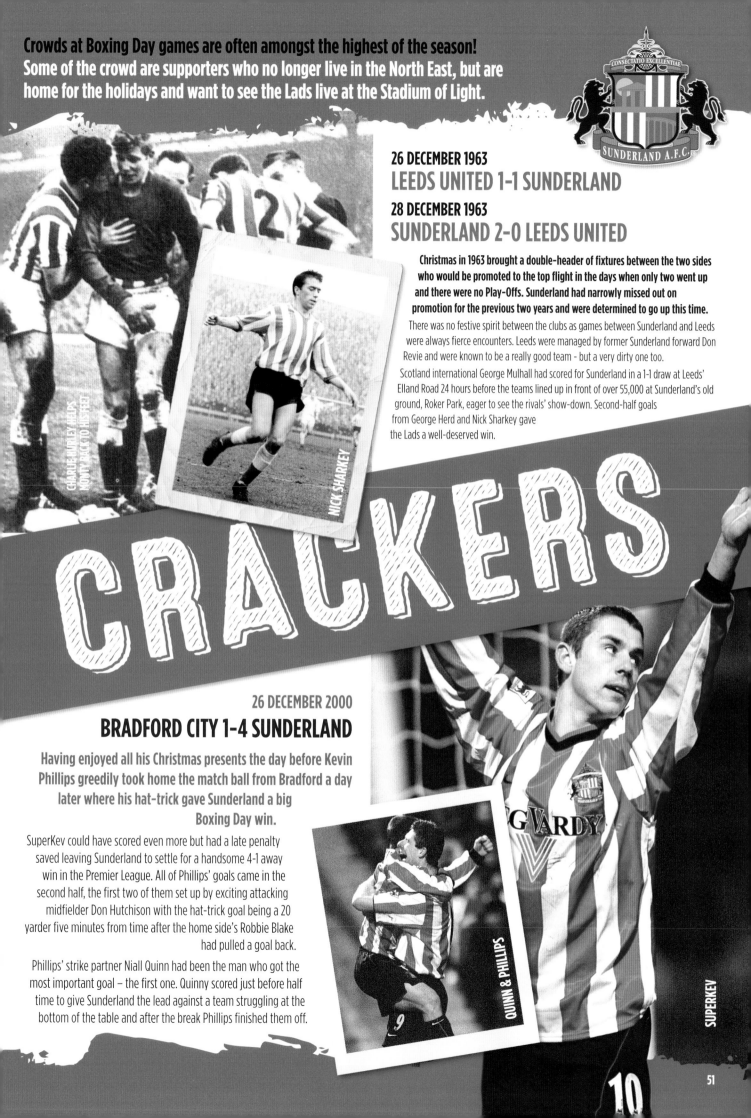

CHARLIE HURLEY HELPS MONTY BACK TO HIS FEET

NICK SHARKEY

26 DECEMBER 1963
LEEDS UNITED 1-1 SUNDERLAND

28 DECEMBER 1963
SUNDERLAND 2-0 LEEDS UNITED

Christmas in 1963 brought a double-header of fixtures between the two sides who would be promoted to the top flight in the days when only two went up and there were no Play-Offs. Sunderland had narrowly missed out on promotion for the previous two years and were determined to go up this time.

There was no festive spirit between the clubs as games between Sunderland and Leeds were always fierce encounters. Leeds were managed by former Sunderland forward Don Revie and were known to be a really good team - but a very dirty one too.

Scotland international George Mulhall had scored for Sunderland in a 1-1 draw at Leeds' Elland Road 24 hours before the teams lined up in front of over 55,000 at Sunderland's old ground, Roker Park, eager to see the rivals' show-down. Second-half goals from George Herd and Nick Sharkey gave the Lads a well-deserved win.

CRACKERS

26 DECEMBER 2000
BRADFORD CITY 1-4 SUNDERLAND

Having enjoyed all his Christmas presents the day before Kevin Phillips greedily took home the match ball from Bradford a day later where his hat-trick gave Sunderland a big Boxing Day win.

SuperKev could have scored even more but had a late penalty saved leaving Sunderland to settle for a handsome 4-1 away win in the Premier League. All of Phillips' goals came in the second half, the first two of them set up by exciting attacking midfielder Don Hutchison with the hat-trick goal being a 20 yarder five minutes from time after the home side's Robbie Blake had pulled a goal back.

Phillips' strike partner Niall Quinn had been the man who got the most important goal – the first one. Quinny scored just before half time to give Sunderland the lead against a team struggling at the bottom of the table and after the break Phillips finished them off.

QUINN & PHILLIPS

SUPERKEV

DIDIER 17
NDONG

MONTY

Jim Montgomery is a Sunderland legend.
Now aged 74 'Monty' still lives in Sunderland where he was born.
He is also still a club ambassador for SAFC and at every home game he works in the West Stand in the biggest suite at the Stadium of Light. It is a room named after him: 'The Montgomery Suite.'

Why is 'the Mighty Jim' such an important person in the football club's history? Well goalkeeper Monty made more than 150 appearances MORE than anyone else in the club's history for starters. He also made the most famous save ever seen at Wembley Stadium. Jim's famous save was actually a double save.

Like Sunderland, Leeds United are a Championship club at the moment, but back in 1973, Leeds were the most feared team in the country. They were a side full of superstars and were the hottest of hot favourites to beat Sunderland. Monty and his teammates made sure they didn't and Jim had as much to do with that as anyone. In the cup final he went full length to make a save from United's Trevor Cherry, but the ball fell to Peter Lorimer. He was known to have the hardest shot in football and now had the goal at his mercy from close range.

However as Lorimer's eyes were lighting up, Monty was already pushing himself off the ground from his first save. As Lorimer lashed the ball and TV commentators were ready to announce the goal, unbelievably 'Jimmy Monty' somehow managed to save it. It was sensational, partly because it was a fantastic save and partly because it was in the FA Cup final. However, supporters who watched Monty regularly knew that the save was typical of Jim.

Week-in week-out, Monty was a goalkeeper who produced spectacular reflex saves. That was why he played a total of 627 games for Sunderland. He didn't get picked year after year from 1961 to 1976 because he made a sensational save in 1973. Monty was sensational on a consistent basis.

A Sunderland supporter himself, Jim Montgomery is Sunderland through and through. You might have to ask grandparents rather than parents about him but you should be proud of him because Monty is a true Made in Sunderland Legend.

MADE IN SUNDERLAND

20 YEARS AT THE

1. What year did the Stadium of Light open?

2. Who was the very first game against?

3. Sunderland beat Manchester City 3-1 in the first league game at the stadium but do you know who scored the first goal?

4. There is only one statue of a real person at the stadium. Do you know who it is?

5. After the first 20 years of the stadium which former England international had made the most appearances at the Stadium of Light?

6. Who has scored the most goals at the Stadium of Light?

7. England have played three full internationals at the Stadium of Light, the first one was in 1999 against which team?

8. Which of the following full international teams have not played at the Stadium of Light: England, Scotland, Australia, Belgium and Turkey?

9. Which of the following performers have not played a concert at the Stadium of Light: Beyonce, One Direction, Take That, Bruce Springsteen, The Rolling Stones and Coldplay?

10. In which season was Darren Bent's famous 'beach-ball' goal against Liverpool?

HOW MUCH DO YOU KNOW ABOUT THE STADIUM OF LIGHT?

11. How many times have SAFC won the Championship since they moved to the Stadium of Light?

12. SAFC totalled over 100 points when they won the Championship in 1999 – with exactly how many?

13. Only one match has ever been abandoned at the Stadium of Light. It was because of snow in a game in 2006. Who were Sunderland playing?

14. Sunderland have played two League Cup semi-finals at the Stadium of Light – against Leicester City and who else?

15. Sunderland started the first 20 years at the Stadium of Light with a former Everton player as manager in Peter Reid, but who was the former Everton manager in charge as the 20th season at the stadium ended?

16. Who was the manager the last time Sunderland won promotion in 2007?

17. Who was Sunderland's top scorer in the 19th and 20th seasons at the Stadium of Light?

18. Who is the only goalkeeper to play over 100 games at the Stadium of Light?

19. SuperKev and which other Kevin are the only two players to appear at the SoL for five different teams?

20. Ten players have made 100 or more appearances at the Stadium of Light. How many can you name?

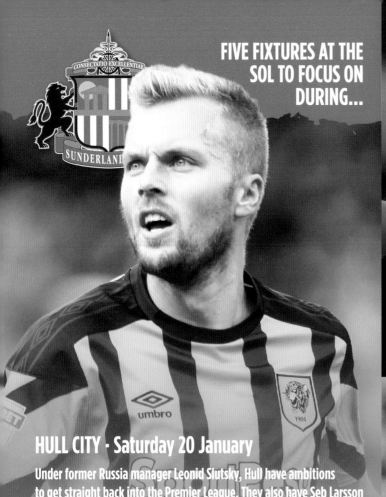

FIVE FIXTURES AT THE SOL TO FOCUS ON DURING...

HULL CITY · Saturday 20 January

Under former Russia manager Leonid Slutsky, Hull have ambitions to get straight back into the Premier League. They also have Seb Larsson who they signed after the Sweden international played over 200 games for Sunderland. There have been some tough tussles with the Tigers in recent years and this one will be a fierce winter's day clash. Wrap up warm!

MIDDLESBROUGH · Saturday 24 February

Star striker Britt Assombalonga cost £15m from Forest and – providing he is fit, as he has had injury worries – will be the man to watch in the Wear-Tees derby. Along with Danish target man Martin Braithwaite, it will be a battle between them and Sunderland's defence and a good test for Tyias Browning. The biggest battle though will be between midfielders Lee Cattermole and Grant Leadbitter – both up against the clubs they supported and played for at the start of their careers.

ASTON VILLA · Tuesday 6 March

Former Sunderland manager Steve Bruce brings a Villa team north likely to be in the thick of the promotion race as the end of the season begins to draw near. With former Chelsea and England man John Terry adding his experience at the back, Villa will be attractive, but difficult opponents as serial promotion winner Bruce looks to put one over on his old club.

PRESTON NORTH END · Saturday 17 March

Simon Grayson was manager of Preston for over three years before leaving the Deepdale club to take over at the Stadium of Light. Every manager likes to win every game, but especially against their old club, so this will add an extra bit of excitement to the match. Preston are now managed by Alex Neil, who when he was manager of Norwich lost a key game at home to SAFC that led to his team being relegated, so he too will have an added reason to want to put one over on the Black Cats.

WOLVES · Saturday 6 May

The last league match of the season and hopefully one with everything to play for. Sunderland will hope to be in the promotion hunt, even if that means playing for a place in the Play-Offs. Wolverhampton Wanderers are also very ambitious. Although they haven't done much in recent years, like Aston Villa and Preston they have had spells where they have been the biggest and most exciting team in the country and their fans want to see a return to the glory days..

THE SECOND HALF OF THE SEASON

JANUARY 2018

Monday	1	Barnsley	H	3.00pm
Saturday	13	Cardiff City	A	3.00pm
Saturday	20	Hull City	H	3.00pm
Saturday	27	Birmingham City	A	3.00pm

FEBRUARY 2018

Saturday	3	Ipswich Town	H	3.00pm
Saturday	10	Bristol City	A	3.00pm
Saturday	17	Brentford	H	3.00pm
Tuesday	20	Bolton Wanderers	A	8.00pm
Saturday	24	Middlesbrough	H	3.00pm

MARCH 2018

Saturday	3	Millwall	A	3.00pm
Tuesday	6	Aston Villa	H	7.45pm
Saturday	10	Queens Park Rangers	A	3.00pm
Saturday	17	Preston North End	H	3.00pm
Friday	30	Derby County	A	7.45pm

APRIL 2018

Monday	2	Sheffield Wednesday	H	3.00pm
Saturday	7	Leeds United	A	3.00pm
Tuesday	10	Norwich City	H	7.45pm
Saturday	14	Reading	A	3.00pm
Saturday	21	Burton Albion	H	3.00pm
Saturday	28	Fulham	A	3.00pm

MAY 2018

Sunday	6	Wolves	H	3.00pm

Fixtures are subject to change.

2017-18 PREDICTIONS

CHAMPIONSHIP

OUR PREDICTION FOR ALSO PROMOTED TO THE PREMIER LEAGUE:

NOTTINGHAM FOREST & NORWICH CITY

YOUR PREDICTION:

OUR WISH FOR EFL SKY BET CHAMPIONSHIP WINNERS:

SUNDERLAND

YOUR PREDICTION:

OUR PREDICTION FOR EMIRATES FA CUP WINNERS:

ARSENAL

YOUR PREDICTION:

FA CUP

IN 2018? ...YOU DECIDE!

PREMIER LEAGUE

OUR PREDICTION FOR PREMIER LEAGUE CHAMPIONS:

MANCHESTER UNITED

YOUR PREDICTION:

OUR PREDICTION FOR PREMIER LEAGUE RUNNERS-UP:

LIVERPOOL

YOUR PREDICTION:

OUR PREDICTION FOR PREMIER LEAGUE BOTTOM THREE:

BOURNEMOUTH, STOKE CITY & NEWCASTLE UTD

YOUR PREDICTION:

OUR PREDICTION FOR CARABAO CUP WINNERS:

MANCHESTER CITY

YOUR PREDICTION:

LEAGUE CUP

GEORGE HONEYMAN

When Prudhoe-born George dinked home the winner at Bury in SAFC's first win under Simon Grayson, it was a goal made at the Sunderland Academy.

It was a first senior goal for Sunderland, by a player who started at the Academy of Light when he was just 10 years old.

Coming under a month before Honeyman's 23rd birthday George's first goal was reward for the hard work of a player who has really developed his game. When Honeyman first started to appear at Under 18 level, he looked like a naturally talented creative player, but perhaps too light-weight to succeed. George has sacrificed none of his skill, his low centre of gravity or his eye for a pass, but in the last 12 months or so he has shown real evidence of sheer hunger to succeed.

The player who once wanted the ball given to him so he could weave his magic, has developed into a player who combines talent with team-work. Fired up to prove he can make it as a first-team player at Sunderland, Honeyman has become a player who always works very hard, chases all over the pitch and really goes into tackles as if he means them. There are no half measures and it is paying off.

Given a very brief debut by Gus Poyet as a late substitute in an FA Cup defeat at Bradford City in February 2015, for a while looked like it might be George's only taste of first-team football. A loan to Gateshead helped add to his desire to do well at Sunderland as he saw football at the other end of the scale in the Conference, but he had to wait until the very last day of the season after his debut to get another chance for the Lads. On that occasion he did himself no harm with a substitute appearance in the Premier League draw at Watford.

Just as he had begun to impress manager Sam Allardyce, George found he had to start again in earning the trust and belief of David Moyes in 2016-17. Half way though that season, he got a chance in the FA Cup against Burnley and went on to make five further appearances before beginning the current campaign with praise from new boss Simon Grayson ringing in his ears.

Hopefully George will continue to progress and having signed a new two-year contract in the summer, it would be terrific to see this local home grown talent become a regular first choice.

MADE IN SUNDERLAND

GEORGE **26**
HONEYMAN

ANSWERS

PAGE 26 · WHO ARE YER?

1. James Vaughan. 2. Lee Cattermole. 3. Aiden McGeady. 4. Donald Love.

5. George Honeyman. 6. Lewis Grabban. 7. Joel Asoro. 8. Brendan Galloway.

9. Didier Ndong.

PAGE 31 · FOOTBALL 50 WORDSEARCH

The missing word is FIXTURE.

PAGE 38 · THE CHAMPIONSHIP CHALLENGE

1. John Terry. 2. Bayern Munich. 3. Steve Bruce. 4. Angus MacDonald. 5. Crystal Palace.

6. Paul Heckingbottom. 7. Craig Gardner. 8. 2011. 9. Jota. 10. Four times.

11. Middlesbrough. 12. Phil Parkinson. 13. 4-1. 14. Neal Maupay. 15. Mark Warburton.

16. Tammy Abraham. 17. Watford. 18. Adam Matthews. 19. Nigel Clough. 20. Liam Boyce.

21. Stephen Warnock. 22. Red. 23. Neil Warnock. 24. Gary Medel. 25. Bradley Johnson.

26. 1946. 27. Tom Huddlestone. 28. Atletico Madrid. 29. Marcus Bettinelli.

30. Tom Cairney. 31. The Tigers. 32. Russia. 33. Arsenal. 34. Joe Garner.

35. Sir Alf Ramsey. 36. 1977-78. 37. Marching On Together. 38. Seven. 39. Liam Cooper.

40. Connor Roberts. 41. Seville. 42. The League Cup. 43. Neil Harris.

44. Manchester United. 45. The Lions. 46. Borussia Dortmund II. 47. Four.

48. Angus Gunn. 49. Newcastle United. 50. True. 51. Liam Bridcutt. 52. Jordan Hugill.

53. David Moyes. 54. Won all four divisions of English football. 55. Nedum Onuoha.

56. Christopher Samba. 57. Martin O'Neill. 58. Jaap Stam,. 59. Third. 60. Vito Mannone.

61. Leon Clarke. 62. 100. 63. Chelsea. 64. George Boyd.

65. 150 years old, they were formed in 1867. 66. 8. 67. Callum McManaman.

68. Three: Aston Villa, Preston North End and Leeds United.

69. George Honeyman and Lynden Gooch. 70. Southampton. 71. Six. 72. Ruben Neves.

PAGE 44 · WORLD CUP QUIZ

1930. Argentina. 1934. Four. 1938. Paris. 1950. USA. 1954. Hungary.

1958 & 1962. Brazil. 1966. World Cup Willie. 1970. Italy.

1974. The Cruyff turn, after legendary Dutch footballer Johan Cruyff. 1978. Mario Kempes.

1982. Norman Whiteside v Yugoslavia, 0-0, 17 June 1982.. 1986. Diego Maradona.

1990. Cameroon. 1994. Russia. 1998. Ronaldo. 2002. Miroslav Klose.

2006. Portugal 1-0 Netherlands. 2010. Jozy Altidore. 2014. Jordan Henderson.

2018. Russia.

PAGE 56 · SOL20 QUIZ

1. 1997. 2. Ajax of Amsterdam. 3. Niall Quinn.

4. Bob Stokoe, the manager of the team who won the FA Cup in 1973.

5. Michael Gray who played at the stadium 125 times for Sunderland and once for Blackburn Rovers.

6. Kevin Philips with 63 - 30 more than the next highest who is Niall Quinn.

7. Belgium. 8. Scotland. 9. The Rolling Stones. 10. 2009-10.

11. Three times: 1999, 2005 and 2007. 12. 105. 13. Fulham. 14. Manchester United.

15. David Moyes. 16. Roy Keane. 17. Jermain Defoe. 18. Thomas Sorensen.

19. Kevin Kilbane.

20. Michael Gray, Kevin Phillips, John O'Shea, Darren Williams, Thomas Sorensen, Seb Larsson, Niall Quinn, Phil Bardsley, Dean Whitehead and Lee Cattermole.